C000156933

▶ CONTENTS ◀

WELCOME TO A FRESH
ADVENTURE WITH GOD

Every day when we go to work we have the opportunity to contribute to the lives of hundreds – sometimes even thousands – of people through the work we do and the organisations we work in. It's an amazing privilege. Still, overall, the contemporary workplace is a more demanding, less secure, and less ethically robust arena than it was ten years ago. In such a context, it's tempting to focus our talking and praying about work on pressure points – problems to solve, crises to avert, targets to meet.

But working with God is about far more than coping.

Working with God is about working with the King of the Universe in his great mission – the reconciliation and renewal of all things – his kingdom come, his will be done on earth as it is in heaven; his kingdom come, his will be done in our workplaces as it is in heaven.

Christians at work, then, are strategically placed to bring biblical values and heartfelt prayers to every task and every relationship and every organisation. Through our work we can play a significant role in changing the way that work gets done for the better – changing the systems, the structures, the products, the services, changing the relationships, the atmosphere... if not in the whole organisation by Tuesday lunchtime, then in our bit of the organisation over time.

Transforming Work is a journey to help make those kinds of changes a reality. It's a journey of seeing work differently and doing work differently, of God at work with us and in us, and in those we work with.

As a journey, *Transforming Work* has an itinerary. There are eight stops along the way to learn new things, review progress, share stories, pray together, plan ahead, and, in between, lots of opportunities to try things out. Along the way, because it is a journey we make with God, unpredictable things are likely to happen – opportunities arise, questions surface, challenges emerge. So *Transforming Work* is designed to be flexible to the needs of a particular group, whilst ensuring that good foundations are laid for the future.

As a leader, we hope and pray that you'll have the delight of seeing people encounter God in fresh ways as you wrestle together with some key questions biblically and practically. We pray too that you will also see the impact on the work they do, the colleagues they work with, and the organisations they work for. In the year you are together and beyond.

So joy, peace, and grace be yours in it all.

Mark Greene & Ruth Walker

LICC

'The primary action of the church in the world is the action of its members in their daily work.'
– Lesslie Newbigin

TRANSFORMING WORK:
▶ 1. AN OVERVIEW ◀

Transforming Work brings together a group of working Christians to form a learning community that meets together for eight sessions spaced over a year. This unique approach leaves space between gatherings to reflect, try things out, and pray, while giving time for seeds to grow, discoveries to be made, and God to work.

The group sessions combine short conversation starter films on workplace issues with skills development, video stories, learning to read the Bible though Workers' Eyes, prayer, lively conversation, and a big helping of good humour! The accompanying app for iOS and Android is packed full of materials to enable each individual participant to prepare for each session, go deeper, track discoveries, and continue the journey between sessions.

WHAT DOES A SESSION LOOK LIKE?

Each session allows participants to reflect on what they have been learning and seeing between sessions, offers a mix of fresh content and activities that take the group deeper, and looks forward to putting this into practice before the next session.

A typical session and rough timings might look like this:

WELCOME & REVIEW   10-15 mins

A time for people to share stories of how they have seen God working in and through them since the last session.

FEEDBACK   20-25 mins

An open time to share thoughts on the work done between sessions.

CORE CONTENT   40-50 mins

The heart of each session, during which key concepts and ideas are introduced on the Table Talk video, followed by extended discussion.

BIBLE THROUGH WORKERS' EYES   20-30 mins

Feeding back on a passage of the Bible together and its implications for workplace situations.

PRAYER   15-20 mins

An opportunity for focused prayer in small groups or pairs.

JOURNEYING ON   5-10 mins

A look forward to the preparation needed for the next session.

To run through a session in full takes between 2 and 2½ hours. But *Transforming Work* is intended to be flexible and serve the needs of the group. So, if you find there is a keen interest in dwelling on a particular issue, please don't feel you have to rush on to complete every element of the session. Use your discernment to guide the group towards what it looks like will be most fruitful, and adjust the time you spend on other elements as necessary.

If you have less than 2 hours, but still want to run *Transforming Work* (e.g. over breakfast), again use your judgement to focus on what is most helpful for the group. All of the elements are beneficial, but you would probably want to make sure that you include at least the following: an opportunity to feedback what's happened in between sessions; a discussion around the core content; and some prayer before making sure everyone knows what they are doing in advance of the next time you meet.

WHAT DOES THE TRANSFORMING WORK RESOURCE COMPRISE?

▶ FOR LEADERS – THE PACK

This Leader's Pack contains all the materials you need to lead a Transforming Work group, including:

- ▶ Session Guides (Section 1)
- ▶ Agendas, exercises, and handouts (Section 2)
- ▶ Getting Going (orientation and tips for leaders – Section 3)

Tip: Visit licc.org.uk/twleaders for access to printable versions of the agendas, exercises and handouts. This also contains materials and information to help you get the group up and running.

- ▶ *Transforming Work* DVD (Table Talk videos, additional session videos, stories, and interviews and training videos)

Tip: This video content is also available online. You can access this content with the code on page 75 by logging in at licc.org.uk/redeem

▶ FOR PARTICIPANTS – THE APP

Each Transforming Work participant will need access to the materials contained within the Transforming Work app. This contains everything they will need to cover between sessions and can be downloaded from the Google Play Store for Android devices and the Apple Store for iOS devices. The app content costs 99p to unlock.

Tip: Group members who do not have an Android or iOS-based device can purchase a web version of the app (also 99p) at licc.org.uk/appaccess

WHAT HAPPENS BETWEEN SESSIONS?

▶ IN-APP MATERIALS

A key part of *Transforming Work* takes place between sessions, where group members put into practice what they have learnt and continue their learning using the multimedia resources on the app. For each session there is material for participants to use in preparation and follow-on exercises to help them go deeper. We also link to a recommended book that can be purchased, though this is optional.

▶ PRAYER PARTNERSHIPS

Another important part of the journey between sessions is meeting with a prayer partner. We've found that this provides people with a valuable opportunity to talk over ideas, pray for specific issues, listen to God, and be mutually accountable. If group members are not part of an existing prayer partnership, we recommend that they form prayer triplets with others in the group. The deep relationships that come from journeying with one another in this way can long outlive the year's programme.

In a typical prayer partnership or triplet meeting you might:

- ▶ Share personal conclusions to questions posed in the preparatory work
- ▶ Share personal experiences of applying what you have learnt together back at work
- ▶ Help each other work on solutions to specific issues
- ▶ Pray for workplace challenges, people, and opportunities

Tip: If you're forming triplets within the group, basing them on things like industry grouping or job role can work well.

▶ JOURNALLING

Group members are encouraged to keep a journal throughout *Transforming Work*. Journalling is a great way of condensing learning, prompting prayer, and keeping track of how things are going at work. There is no one way to journal and each person will have their own preference e.g. notebook, smartphone, or tablet.

WHAT IS MY ROLE AS A GROUP LEADER?

Sessions are best facilitated by one or two working people who accompany the group on their journey by listening, steering discussion, and setting the pace, but not teaching from the front.

Your role will help group members discover that:

- ▶ God values the work they do
- ▶ They have an amazing opportunity to live out and share the good news of God's kingdom at work
- ▶ There is a range of tools to help them do just that

As a group leader you will get to see people's eyes opened to God in their everyday working lives, watch them become confident in the power of the gospel at work in their workplace, and hear their stories of God at work: changing them and changing those around them.

It is our prayer that this journey will transform the way that you see your own work and its part in God's mission, that it will transform the way you read the Bible as you see its wisdom for everyday working life, and that it will transform and expand your view of God as he works in and through you and the people in your group.

▶ 2. STARTING WELL ◀

As with most things worth doing, there is a little bit of work involved in getting a group up and running. The rewards are more than worth it. We've provided some materials on the website (licc.org.uk/twleaders) which you might find helpful in recruiting and setting up a group:

- ▶ Promotional video
- ▶ A commendation video for church leaders
- ▶ Printable posters & flyers
- ▶ Web/newsletter advert
- ▶ Outline for a discovery session

The promotional video is a great introduction to *Transforming Work* and the commendation video will highlight the benefits of the resource for church leaders, encouraging them to support the group. So, if you are planning to run *Transforming Work* in a church context, do talk it over with and gain the support of your church leader.

Encouraging people to download the app is a great way to get them enthused about *Transforming Work*. The app contains a free video (**Work: The Bigger Picture**) which you can use to get people thinking about the ways in which God can work, and is already working, in and through them in their daily contexts.

In addition to this, there's an outline for a simple discovery session in which you can gather interested people for an informal session to explain in more detail how *Transforming Work* works.

WHEN AND WHERE SHOULD WE MEET AS A GROUP?

We recommend you spread the eight sessions over the course of a full calendar year. Put the first two sessions no more than a month apart, so as to generate momentum, but after that, meet every 4-6 weeks with breaks over holiday periods. Get the eight dates in people's diaries at the beginning of the year to help the group commit to the full programme.

Since its launch, *Transforming Work* has been used in many different ways: with friends over brunch on a Saturday or breakfast before work; single or multiple church based groups meeting in homes or centrally; and even a group on an oil rig in the North Sea.

So the location and format of each session will be determined by the needs of your group. But remember that you will need to be able to play the core content videos and story clips wherever you choose to meet. If English is not your first language, you might find the subtitles on the DVD helpful.

▶ 3. PREPARING FOR THE SESSIONS ◀

You probably already have the skills you need to run a *Transforming Work* group really well. There are a few distinctive features of *Transforming Work* (e.g. Bible through Workers' Eyes) that might be less familiar, so we've prepared a few short videos and exercises and also some Q&As to help you make the most of the experience. They are great to run through with other *Transforming Work* group leaders or a co-leader, if you have one. Even if you complete them all in one go, they won't take more than a couple of hours. The videos are on the *Transforming Work* DVD. Please go to Section 3: Getting Going (page 65) for information on how to get the most out of these videos.

WHERE CAN I FIND ALL THE RESOURCES I NEED?

All the resources you need are in this Leader's Pack – in the printed guide or on the DVD. The enclosed *Transforming Work* DVD contains all the videos you will need to play in the session – both core content and stories. All other agendas, exercises, and handouts can be found in Section 2.

Tip: Printable versions of these are also available at licc.org.uk/twleaders. Exercises and handouts are provided in-app for group members who prefer to complete them digitally.

'We have a purpose, we have a sacred calling, we have a God-given vocation: to partner with God in his work of restoring all things. What could be more exhilarating than that?'
- Amy Sherman, *Kingdom Calling*

SECTION 1

SESSION GUIDES

·SESSION 1·

WHY DOES WORK MATTER?

SESSION 1:
WHY DOES WORK MATTER?

This first session is a chance to look at the big picture and consider why work is so important to God. As the introduction to *Transforming Work*, this session is unusual in that it includes two core content videos. The first (Work: The Big Picture) helps to set the scene by laying out a vision for Christians at work. The second video (Where Have You Seen God at Work?) introduces a framework for fruitful discipleship using the 6Ms. People in your group may be more or less familiar with this material, so feel free to be flexible with how much time you spend on each section. The goal is that by the end of the session everyone is on the same page and has a good foundation for the rest of the programme.

SESSION OBJECTIVES

1. To establish the tone and rhythm of the *Transforming Work* group sessions

2. To enable the group to understand and articulate a biblical vision for work

3. To equip the group to use the 6M framework to see what God is doing at work

SESSION MATERIALS

▶ *Transforming Work* DVD for Work: The Bigger Picture, Table Talk, and Bible through Workers' Eyes videos
▶ Copies of Session 1 agenda
▶ M&M sweets (you may like to bring some to connect to the 6Ms)

GROUP INTRODUCTIONS   25 mins

Introduce yourself, giving a brief history of your working background and motivation for being part of *Transforming Work*.

Ask each group member to:

▶ Introduce themselves and their workplace contexts
▶ Give a brief summary of the opportunities and challenges they currently face at work
▶ Share their hopes for the *Transforming Work* journey

Tip: You will find it useful to make a few notes at this stage as it will help you initiate and guide future conversations.

HOW THE GROUP WILL OPERATE   10 mins

Take a moment to highlight the core values of *Transforming Work* (on the next page) to help the group get the most out of the process.

Check that everyone has downloaded the *Transforming Work* app and unlocked the course content. Explain that the app provides the material for use between sessions, which is a key part of the journey.

Decide on a way to keep in touch between sessions (e.g. Email, WhatsApp, private Facebook group).

Tip: Group members who do not have a device that can run Android or iOS based apps can be given access to these key resources online by emailing tw@licc.org.uk.

HELPFUL CORE VALUES

Commitment ▶ People need to be ready to commit not only to group sessions but also to personal reflection, prayer, and applying the learning between sessions.

Co-learning ▶ Everyone has something to give. By sharing openly you will learn from one another, through your successes and failures.

Confidentiality ▶ What is shared in the group stays in the group.

CORE CONTENT: WORK: THE BIGGER PICTURE   20 mins

Watch Work: The Bigger Picture (8.5 mins)

Discuss the vision, using some of the following questions:

▶ What was new, challenging, or inspiring?
▶ What struck you from this vision when thinking about your own work?
▶ What difference does it make to your attitude to work?

CORE CONTENT: SEEING GOD AT WORK   30 mins

Watch Where Have You Seen God at Work? (12 mins)

Each session from now on will start with this question (see the 6M framework below). Give the group an opportunity to share any initial observations.

Invite the group to discuss in pairs and then share which two Ms they feel are most visible in their life at work and which two are the least.

▶ What themes has the group observed?

Tip: You don't need to unpack the 6Ms in detail at this stage as most will be revisited in future sessions.

Encourage the group to use the 6M framework in the coming weeks to help them develop 'eyes to see' what God is doing in their daily work, and to come ready to share at the next session.

THE 6M FRAMEWORK

The 6M framework (see page 44) offers six different ways in which we can be fruitful for Jesus, helping the group build a broad picture of Christian living that includes, but also goes beyond, verbal witness. It isn't another holy to-do list but a way to help the group have eyes to see the ways in which they have already been fruitful for Christ, as well as stirring their imagination for the rich range of ways God might work through them.

Each session from now on starts with the key question 'Where have you seen God at work?' to encourage the group to share stories, and the 6Ms can be a useful lens to help them see what God has been doing. Over time, this will become one of the most significant parts of each session.

Tip: Those who have completed *Fruitfulness on the Frontline* will already be familiar with the 6M framework. The core video frames this specifically for a workplace context, so the group might still find it valuable to watch.

PRAYER 15 mins

Spend time praying for one another in light of what has been discussed. Perhaps break into pairs or triplets in order to pray with greater focus.

The following questions will help the group pray with one another for the areas of fruitful living highlighted by the 6Ms:

▶ What can I pray for you personally? (Modelling Godly Character)

▶ What can I pray for your current workload? (Making Good Work)

▶ What can I pray for your colleagues/clients? (Ministering Grace and Love)

▶ What can I pray for your workplace? (Moulding Culture)

▶ Are there any issues of gossip and politicking in your workplace at present? (Mouthpiece for Truth and Justice)

▶ Whose salvation could I pray for? (Messenger of the Gospel)

BIBLE THROUGH WORKERS' EYES 5 mins

Allowing God's word to shape our responses to the opportunities and challenges we face at work is an important part of growing as whole-life disciples of Christ. So learning to look at a passage of the Bible with alertness to its impact on our working lives is a vital part of *Transforming Work*.

Watch Bible through Workers' Eyes Trailer (5 mins)

Alert the group to the audio podcast on the app to help them reflect on each session's passage and prepare to discuss it together in the next session.

JOURNEYING ON 5 mins

▶ Confirm the date for Sessions 2, 3, and 4

▶ Remind people of the material to cover between sessions (see below)

▶ Encourage people to keep a personal journal between sessions (using a notebook or smartphone) to aid reflective thought and help them see how God might be working through them as they try to put things into practice

▶ Ensure that every group member has prayer support in place either though a pre-existing prayer partnership or by creating prayer triplets with other *Transforming Work* group members

SESSION 1: GOING DEEPER

PRAY	Pray using the 6M prayer questions on the app in your triplets or prayer partnerships	Ongoing
WATCH	Jay's Story. Which of the 6Ms can you identify in the story?	5 mins
READ	*Fruitfulness on the Frontline* by Mark Greene (optional)	

SESSION 2: PREPARING

EXERCISE	How Are You Doing at Work?	30 mins
LISTEN	Bible through Workers' Eyes: Ruth & Boaz	5 mins
READ	Ruth 2, noting any features that relate to a workplace situation	30 mins
READ	Another Day, Another Dime by Mark Greene	20 mins
REFLECT	Where have you seen God at work? Use the 6M framework to help you see where God is at work in your everyday situations.	

 13

· SESSION 2 ·

HOW CAN I DO GOOD WORK?

SESSION 2:
HOW CAN I DO GOOD WORK?

One of the most important, yet sometimes most difficult, things to grasp is how the actual work we do can be good in God's eyes. This session helps us build a picture of what good work looks like and how our own work can be done well in worship and service to God. It also helps us wrestle with the question of the significance of our particular job to God.

SESSION OBJECTIVES

1 To gain a biblical perspective on good work

2 To understand how the particular work we do has value to God

3 To practise reading an Old Testament story with alertness to our workplace context

SESSION MATERIALS

▶ *Transforming Work* DVD for Table Talk video
▶ Copies of Session 2 agenda
▶ Quality Street chocolates (to connect to quality work)

WELCOME & REVIEW   15 mins

Ask the group to share their reflections on their work since you last met:

▶ Where have you seen God at work?
This is a key question to help people begin to recognise that God is at work in their everyday. We ask this question in every session to help people to gradually become aware of God at work. Some may find this difficult to begin with, and it may help to use some of the following supplementary questions:

   ▶ Have you seen any of the 6Ms at work?
   ▶ Did you sense God with you in a situation? (Describe it)
   ▶ Did you come across an unexpected solution to a problem?
   ▶ Did you have any specific conversations about your faith?

▶ How did Session 1 affect how you view your work?

FEEDBACK - HOW ARE YOU DOING AT WORK EXERCISE   25 mins

Encourage the group to share their reflections from the exercise.
Ask each member to share their one 'Big Question' for the year.

Tip: Making a note of each participant's 'Big Question' will help you in Session 7 and may help in guiding discussion through the course.

CORE CONTENT: DOING GOOD WORK 　　　　　　　50 mins

Watch How Can I Do Good Work? (12 mins)

Use the questions below to discuss the key points:

1. Good work – in God's ways (Genesis 1)

God's purpose was to create a context in which people could flourish.

▶ Can you see how the goods or services produced through your work help others to flourish?

As God created, he brought order out of chaos, worked in a rhythm of creation and rest, made provision, produced joy, created beauty, and released potential.

▶ How are these characteristics of God's work reflected in your own work?

Our rebellion at the Fall damaged our key relationships with God, each other, our work, and creation itself. Jesus' work of salvation through the cross offers a measure of healing, and our work can be instrumental in that.

▶ Can you see ways in which your work can bring healing and restoration where God's world has been damaged?

2. Good work – in God's strength (Deuteronomy 8:17-18)

Right from the point of creation, the 'breath of God' – his inspiration – has been available for people who work in his service – in all sorts of work.

▶ What difference does God's Holy Spirit make to your work and through you to others at work?

3. Good work – to God's glory (Matthew 5:16)

When people know we follow Christ they will view our work through that lens – positively or negatively. Therefore the way we work - not only the quality but our attitude - should reflect Christ's character. Our prayer, like Jesus' statement, is that people would see beyond the work we do to the God we serve.

▶ What sort of opportunities might you have to point others towards God through the work you do?
▶ Overall, can you see why your particular work is important to God?

BIBLE THROUGH WORKERS' EYES – RUTH & BOAZ 　　　20 mins

Our first passage of Old Testament narrative, Ruth 2, is set 'in the days when the Judges ruled' (Ruth 1:1) – a time of general moral decline and appalling acts of violence in Israel. As such, Boaz stands out as an example of an honest farmer committed to living under God's law.

Ruth Chapter 2
▶ What struck people from their reading and reflection?
▶ What did they spot as they imagined themselves within the story, particularly in the roles of Ruth, Boaz, or his workers?
▶ How might this encourage them to walk with God in their own workplace situations?

Possible additional questions:
▶ How does the story of Boaz stand in contrast to the general trend we see in Judges? What might this teach us about being counter-cultural in our workplaces today?
▶ What can we learn from the way Boaz ran his family business? e.g. how Boaz treated his workforce (especially the women and immigrants), his approach to profit and wider social responsibility?
▶ How do you think that the work Ruth was able to find could be 'good work'?
▶ In what ways is Boaz an example for working people today?

PRAYER   15 mins

Pray for one another in light of this session. In particular, encourage people to bring the Big Questions they identified before God as they pray together.

JOURNEYING ON   5 mins

▶ Confirm the date for Sessions 3, 4, and 5
▶ Remind people of the work to be done between sessions
▶ Encourage people to continue using a personal journal between sessions
▶ Ensure that group members have functioning prayer support in place

SESSION 2: GOING DEEPER

WATCH	▶	Sarah's Story, observing how she works in God's ways	5 mins
WATCH	▶	Sheona's Story, noting how God prepared her for good work	5 mins
READ	🌐	*Every Good Endeavour* by Tim Keller and Katherine Leary Alsdorf (optional)	

SESSION 3: PREPARING

EXERCISE	✎	How Well are you Flourishing? Note that you will need 5 to 10 minutes of help from a close friend/spouse to complete this.	20 mins
WATCH	▶	Marion's Story, noting God's interest in her work	5 mins
LISTEN	🔊	Bible through Workers' Eyes: Joseph	5 mins
READ	📖	Genesis 39-45, with alertness to the workplace	40 mins
REFLECT	✎	Where have you seen God at work? (Use the 6M framework to help you.)	

'The gospel reminds us that God cares about the products we make, the companies we work for, and the customers we serve. He not only loves us, but he also loves the world and wants us to serve it well. My work is a critical way in which God is caring for human beings and renewing his world.'

– Katherine Leary Alsdorf, *Every Good Endeavour*

· S E S S I O N 3 ·

HOW CAN I FLOURISH AT WORK?

SESSION 3:
HOW CAN I FLOURISH AT WORK?

It's tempting to derive our sense of purpose and meaning from a fulfilling or 'respected' job, or to be demotivated by one that falls short of our hopes and dreams. By focusing on our identity as children of God, we can gain a fresh perspective on an integrated life that helps us to flourish as we are grounded in God in every context, including work.

SESSION OBJECTIVES

1. To explore our identity in Christ
2. To see how that helps us to flourish in doing our work for him
3. To further explore reading Old Testament stories through workers' eyes

SESSION MATERIALS

▶ *Transforming Work* DVD for Table Talk videos
▶ Copies of Session 3 agenda
▶ Fruit Pastilles (just for fun, to connect to fruitfulness)

WELCOME & REVIEW   15 mins

Ask the group to share:

▶ Where have you seen God at work? (Additional prompts on page 15)
▶ Have you seen any of the 6Ms at work?

FEEDBACK – 'HOW WELL ARE YOU FLOURISHING' EXERCISE 25 mins

Briefly recap the purpose of this exercise: to take space to reflect; to grow self-awareness; and to gather a snapshot to refer back to in later weeks.

Allow each group member to share reflections and learning points from the exercise. The following questions may be helpful:

▶ What did you learn about yourself?
▶ Where are the challenges for the year ahead?

CORE CONTENT: FLOURISHING AT WORK   40 mins

Ask the group to spend a few minutes writing down how they would describe the role of a Christian at work, then ask for some feedback.

Watch How Can I Flourish at Work? (8 mins)

Follow up the video by asking how being a daughter or son of God at work might change the job description the group wrote down. In discussing their answers, you might explore some of the questions below:

In Paul's letters to the Colossians and the Ephesians he encouraged both masters and slaves to think of God as their ultimate boss. How does an understanding of our identity as sons or daughters of God affect...

- ▶ our view of God as our boss?
- ▶ how we respond to our workplace boss?
- ▶ our sense of Kingdom purpose at work?
- ▶ how we respond when things go wrong?
- ▶ how we view jobs we might not think are ideal?
- ▶ how we use authority where we have been given it?

BIBLE THROUGH WORKERS' EYES - JOSEPH   20 mins

This passage is another story from the Old Testament. Joseph's personal experience is part of God's bigger plan for the people of God and his purposes for all creation and its redemption.

Genesis 39-45
- ▶ What struck the group through their reading and reflection?
- ▶ What connections did they make with their own working lives?

Possible additional questions:
- ▶ How did Joseph use the skills and gifts God gave him in his various roles? What opportunities do you see to use your own God-given abilities?
- ▶ What workplace temptations did Joseph face, and how did he deal with them?
- ▶ Can you learn anything from this about how you might deal with such temptations?
- ▶ Can you learn anything from the way in which Joseph handled setbacks?
- ▶ How did Joseph work in God's image (reflecting God's purpose and heart), in his strength (inspired by God's Holy Spirit), and to his glory (in a way that pointed to God)?
- ▶ What is God doing in the story? (look at Ch. 45 and 50:20)
- ▶ What was the key to Joseph's success?

PRAYER   15 mins

Get the group to pray for one another in light of all that has been discussed.

You may find it helpful to use the model below:

▶ **Pressure Points** – What pressures are you and your colleagues facing at home or at work? Take this opportunity to be real amongst others who are well positioned to understand some of the challenges you face.

▶ **Kingdom Purpose** – What do you sense is God's heart for your workplace and those you work alongside right now? What is the most strategic area you feel God is calling you to focus on? This is a chance for you to recognise what God is already doing in and through you as his children at work, to ask for his favour, and to discern what else he might do.

JOURNEYING ON   5 mins

▶ Confirm the date for Sessions 4, 5, and 6
▶ Remind people of the material to cover between sessions
▶ Ask how the group is getting on with keeping personal journals
▶ Ask how prayer partnerships between sessions are working

SESSION 3: GOING DEEPER

WATCH    Living an Integrated Life, an interview with Paul Valler   5 mins

READ   *Get a Life* by Paul Valler (optional)

SESSION 4: PREPARING

LISTEN   Bible through Workers' Eyes: Jehoshaphat   5 mins

READ   2 Chronicles 17–20, thinking about how Jehoshaphat went about influencing the   40 mins
                                culture in Judah through his role as ruler

WATCH   Anita's Story, looking out for her influence on workplace culture   5 mins

REFLECT   Where have you seen God at work?

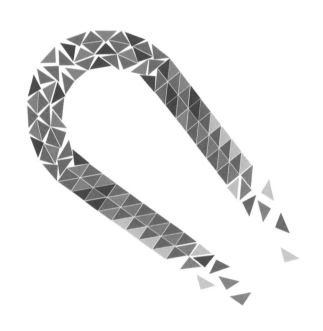

·SESSION 4·

HOW CAN I INFLUENCE THE CULTURE OF MY WORKPLACE?

SESSION 4:
HOW CAN I INFLUENCE THE CULTURE OF MY WORKPLACE?

One description of culture is 'the way we do things around here'. Every workplace culture is different and beneath the outward expression of culture (behaviour, policies, general practice etc.) is a set of core beliefs and values (e.g. valuing loyalty, profit, or teamwork).

By being attentive to the values that drive culture in our own workplaces we can, through both prayer and action, seek to influence the way things are done there with God's help.

SESSION OBJECTIVES

1 ▸ To equip the group to diagnose and influence their workplace culture

2 ▸ To consolidate reading Old Testament narrative with alertness to the workplace

SESSION MATERIALS

▸ *Transforming Work* DVD for Table Talk and Chris' Story videos

▸ Copies of Session 4 agenda

▸ Copies of 'Exploring the Culture of my Workplace' exercise

▸ Chocolate biscuits (connects to Anita's Story)

WELCOME & REVIEW   15 mins

Ask the group to share what God has been teaching them since you last met together:

▸ Where have you seen God at work?
▸ Have you seen any of the 6Ms at work?

FEEDBACK – LIVING AN INTEGRATED LIFE INTERVIEW   25 mins

Invite the group to share reflections on the interview with Paul Valler:

▸ What did you find encouraging or challenging in Paul's view of living an integrated life?
▸ What implications did it have for you?

'Culture is the ensemble of stories we tell each other about ourselves.'
– Clifford Geertz

BIBLE THROUGH WORKERS' EYES – JEHOSHAPHAT   20 mins

After Solomon's reign the nation of Israel split into two: Israel in the North and Judah in the South. Each was ruled by a succession of kings, some of whom, like David, were true to God, but many of whom were rebellious and self-serving.

Jehoshaphat succeeded his father Asa as King of Judah, which at that time was vulnerable to invasion both from the northern kingdom Israel, and from its hostile neighbours. He not only addressed the security of Israel, but also sought to influence its culture for the better. We may not all have the sort of power that Jehoshaphat had as king, but in some way we can all influence the culture of our workplaces, even if it's just in our corner.

2 Chronicles 17-20
- ▶ What struck the group from their reading and reflection?
- ▶ How did Jehoshaphat go about changing the culture for the better?
- ▶ What was Jehoshaphat's first responsibility when he took over, and what did he do?
- ▶ What core beliefs and core values shaped Jehoshaphat's actions?

Possible additional questions:
- ▶ What can you learn from Jehoshaphat's approach that could help you to promote kingdom values amongst your own colleagues?
- ▶ What do you see God doing through Jehoshaphat's reign?

CORE CONTENT: INFLUENCING WORKPLACE CULTURE   40 mins

Ask the group to try question 1 on the What's the Culture of my Workplace? exercise in pairs. This is an easy way in to start thinking about the culture of our organisations and should provide some interesting feedback.

Ask the group to work individually on question 2.

Reflecting on the answers to these two questions can give the group some insight into the values they experience in their workplaces, so before watching the video ask the group to try question 3.

Watch How Can I Influence the Culture of my Workplace? (11 mins)

Some of the values in our workplaces will be in line with God's ways and we will want to affirm and champion them. Other values will stand in conflict with kingdom values, and it is here that we can prayerfully look to influence for the better.

Explore questions 4 and 5. The aim here is to move from discerning workplace values to looking at how they match up with biblical values, and then to identify some concrete first steps towards influencing our workplace culture for the better.

We're not going to be able to transform our entire workplace culture at once. We can, however, always look for small things to influence. These 'one-degree shifts' can gradually reshape our workplace culture.

Watch Chris' Story (3 mins)

This story describes a significant change in workplace policy.
- ▶ Looking at how Chris approached the issue, why do you think he was ultimately successful?

PRAYER 15 mins

Pray for one another in light of what has been discussed in the session.

Pray for the one-degree shifts that people have identified, asking for God's strength and wisdom as people seek to try them out.

Tip: If people have found it hard to identify one-degree shifts, suggest they spend time asking God for insight while remaining open to what he may ask them to do.

JOURNEYING ON 5 mins

▸ Confirm the date for Sessions 5, 6, and 7
▸ Remind people of the work to be done between sessions
▸ Encourage people to keep journalling and praying

SESSION 4: GOING DEEPER

DO	One-degree shifts in your workplace (as identified in 'What's the Culture of my Workplace?')	Daily
WATCH	'Counter-Cultural Working' interview with Jago Wynne	5 mins
READ	William's Story	10 mins
READ	*Culture Making* by Andy Crouch (optional)	

SESSION 5: PREPARING

LISTEN	Bible through Workers' Eyes: Over To You	20 mins
READ	Your regular Bible passages, but with a specific alertness to your workplace context	5 mins
REFLECT	Where have you seen God at work?	Daily

'...What the Holy Spirit unleashed through the first Christians was nothing less than a cultural revolution...the culture they created was so attractive that by the fourth century A.D., an entire empire was on the verge of faith.'
– Andy Crouch, *Culture Making*

·SESSION 5·

HOW CAN I IMPROVE RELATIONSHIPS AT WORK?

SESSION 5:
HOW CAN I IMPROVE
RELATIONSHIPS AT WORK?

Almost everything we do at work will have a relational element – we cannot get things done without relationships. More than this though, living and working in relationship with one another is how we were designed to operate. Looking at issues through a 'relational lens' is a deeply biblical principle.

When problems arise at work, we can often be quick to find a pragmatic solution without stopping to think whether (directly or indirectly) there might be a relational root to the issue. By learning to think relationally, we can often bring a godly solution to bear and be more effective.

SESSION OBJECTIVES

1 To assess our key workplace relationships

2 To provide tools that help us to improve our relationships at work

3 To encourage one another in reading the Bible through workers' eyes

SESSION MATERIALS

▸ *Transforming Work* DVD for Table Talk and Laura's Story videos
▸ Copies of Session 5 agenda
▸ Copies of 'How are My Workplace Relationships?' exercise
▸ Jelly Babies (to connect with people)

WELCOME & REVIEW   15 mins

Ask the group to share reflections since the last session:

▸ Where have you seen God at work?
▸ What has God been teaching you through your work since last time?

FEEDBACK - MAKING ONE-DEGREE SHIFTS   25 mins

Invite the group to share reflections on making some one-degree shifts in workplace culture:

▸ Are there any stories of change, or 'green shoots' that we can celebrate and praise God for?
▸ Has anyone had any further ideas that they have not yet had time to try out?
▸ Have there been any obstacles or resistance to suggested changes at work? Could the group brainstorm possible solutions and pray?

BIBLE THROUGH WORKERS' EYES - OVER TO YOU   20 mins

The group will have been trying out their skills in reading the Bible through workers' eyes in their own devotional Bible reading since last time.

Ask the group to feedback on their experiences. Try to tease out not only biblical insights into work, but also anything they found particularly helpful or difficult in this exercise.

Here are some specific questions to help the discussion if necessary:

- What insights for your workplaces did you gain from the Bible?
- What types of biblical literature did you read?
- Which parts of the Bible were easier to connect to your work?
- How did you feel about the exercise overall?

CORE CONTENT: IMPROVING WORKPLACE RELATIONSHIPS   40 mins

To start the discussion around relational thinking, ask the following questions:

- What do the two 'greatest commandments' in Mark 12:29-31 tell us about God's heart for relationships at work?
- Are there any issues in your workplace that could have a relational root?

Give each group member a copy of the exercise How are My Workplace Relationships? Ask them to complete the 'quick three-step health check' (question 1 a-c) before watching the Table Talk video.

Watch How Can I Improve Relationships at Work? **(12.5 mins)**

Afterwards, use question 2 on the exercise to explore how workplace relationships could be improved. It can be helpful to do the first part of this question together as a group, but make sure that each member has an opportunity to think about and write down some specific actions after the discussion.

If you have time...

Watch Laura's story **(2.5 mins)**

- What struck you about the ways in which Laura went about 'loving her neighbour' at work?

'You can't even make money without effective relationships, because markets and companies are, in the end, only groups of people working together.'
- Michael Schluter & David John Lee, *The Relational Manager*

PRAYER
15 mins

Spend some time praying for one another in light of what has been discussed. Perhaps break into small groups or pairs in order to pray with more focus.

Pray for specific workplace relationships (perhaps some of those identified in the exercise).

JOURNEYING ON
5 mins

- ▶ Confirm the date for Sessions 6, 7, and 8
- ▶ Remind people of the work to be done between sessions
- ▶ Encourage the group to continue with personal journals and prayer between sessions

SESSION 5: GOING DEEPER

DO	Specific steps towards improving your workplace relationships (as identified in 'How are my Workplace Relationships?')	Ongoing
WATCH	Mel's Story, looking out for what she brings to workplace relationships	5 mins
WATCH	John's Story (1)	5 mins
READ	Life Through the Relational Lens by Mark Greene	20 mins
READ	*The Relational Manager* by Michael Schluter and David John Lee (optional)	

SESSION 6: PREPARING

LISTEN	Bible through Workers' Eyes: Jesus & his Disciples	5 mins
READ	John 1:29-51 with alertness to introducing others to Jesus	30 mins
WATCH	Neil's Stories	5 mins
WATCH	Victor's Story (1)	5 mins
REFLECT	Where have you seen God at work?	

'The real battles of faith today are being fought in factories, shops, offices & farms, in political parties and government agencies, in countless homes, in press, radio & television, in the relationship of nations. Very often it is said the Church should go into the spheres but the fact is that the Church is already in those spheres in the persons of the laity.'
- World Council of Churches, 1954

29

›SESSION 6‹

HOW CAN I SHARE MY FAITH AT WORK?

SESSION 6:
HOW CAN I SHARE MY FAITH AT WORK?

Many Christians carry emotional 'baggage' when it comes to evangelism at work and can feel guilty at their perceived lack of fruitfulness. Often we only consider it to be success when we get a clear opportunity to share the gospel or when someone becomes a Christian, and we discount steps along the way that are important for the people we work with.

Of course, every workplace is different. Some are in places where relationships are easy to develop and some people can find themselves in environments so hostile that it puts them off any direct conversation about faith.

In either instance it's easy to get bogged down by the hurdles we see, the questions we fear being asked, or our own fears. However, we know God wants people saved so this session focuses on people, not problems.

SESSION OBJECTIVES

1 To gain confidence in talking about Jesus with colleagues, building on the relational thinking from Session 5

2 To equip the group with practical ways of witnessing in a workplace context

3 To practise reading a gospel story with an alertness to the workplace

SESSION MATERIALS

▶ *Transforming Work* DVD for Table Talk videos
▶ Copies of Session 6 agenda
▶ Copies of 'Intentional Steps: Sharing Faith' exercise
▶ A big bar of chocolate to share

WELCOME & REVIEW   15 mins

Ask the group to share reflections since the last session:

▶ Where have you seen God at work?
▶ Which of the 6Ms have been in play?
▶ What has God been teaching you through your work since last time?

FEEDBACK – IMPROVING WORKPLACE RELATIONSHIPS   25 mins

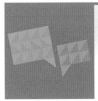

Gather feedback on steps taken to strengthen relationships:

▶ How did Session 5 affect the way you treat your workplace relationships?
▶ What practical steps did you take and what effects have they had?

CORE CONTENT: SHARING YOUR FAITH AT WORK   40 mins

Ask the group to think back to the significant workplace relationships they identified in the last session, and prayerfully consider which of those people God might want to nudge along their journey closer towards himself. For the purposes of this session, ask them to pick one person on whom to focus and to answer the first four questions on the Intentional Steps: Sharing Faith exercise before playing the Table Talk video.

Watch How Can I Share my Faith At Work? **(15 mins)**

Lead a discussion after the video that grounds these ideas in the group's workplace contexts. You might find some of the following questions helpful:

▶ Can you discern where the person you identified earlier is on their journey? What sort of interaction would be appropriate at this point?
▶ Looking at your answers to the first four questions in the exercise, what sort of initiatives could deepen your relationship? (The ideas we looked at in the previous session could help here)
▶ What are the 'high opportunity moments' in the rhythm of your workplace?
▶ What kind of gospel perspectives could work well in your context?
▶ Where the environment is hostile to direct evangelism, think back to Neil's stories that you watched in preparation for this session. How might some of those strategies work in your context?
▶ In what ways can you provide 'pathways forward' to help your colleague in their spiritual journey?

Ask the group to pray together (see below) and, after that, to use the remaining part of the 'Intentional Steps' exercise to consider and record some actions.

PRAYER   15 mins

Spend some time in twos or threes asking God for discernment for your colleagues:

▶ What is God doing in their lives?
▶ Where are they on their journey?
▶ What might be a helpful next step?

Use the 'Intentional Steps' exercise to record any insights and decide on some concrete actions.

'With each individual, I try to see where I fit into God's plan for bringing that person to Christ.'
– Larry Moyer, *Personal Evangelism*

BIBLE THROUGH WORKERS' EYES – JESUS & HIS DISCIPLES 20 mins

Our gospel passage comes at the beginning of Jesus' ministry as he is gathering his first disciples. The narrative gives us some insight into the different ways in which these early disciples were introduced to Jesus. This passage is different to earlier sessions in that there is no explicit connection with work in the story, but the passage includes a disciple of Jesus dealing with a sceptical man. So how might this account help us in today's workplace?

John 1:29-51
▶ What struck the group from their reading and reflections?

Possible additional questions:
▶ In what different ways are these first disciples introduced to Jesus?
▶ What can we learn from the role that these early disciples played in connecting others with Jesus?
▶ Discuss any insights about introducing colleagues to Jesus that this passage raises.
▶ Why do you think the 'messengers' chose the people they did?

'Most Christians can name a number of people who served as links in the chain of their spiritual journey to Christ.'
– Bill Peel & Walt Larimore, *Workplace Grace*

JOURNEYING ON   5 mins

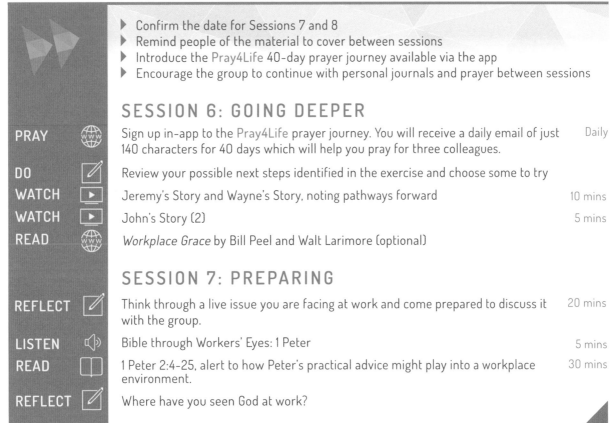

▶ Confirm the date for Sessions 7 and 8
▶ Remind people of the material to cover between sessions
▶ Introduce the Pray4Life 40-day prayer journey available via the app
▶ Encourage the group to continue with personal journals and prayer between sessions

SESSION 6: GOING DEEPER

PRAY	Sign up in-app to the Pray4Life prayer journey. You will receive a daily email of just 140 characters for 40 days which will help you pray for three colleagues.	Daily
DO	Review your possible next steps identified in the exercise and choose some to try	
WATCH	Jeremy's Story and Wayne's Story, noting pathways forward	10 mins
WATCH	John's Story (2)	5 mins
READ	*Workplace Grace* by Bill Peel and Walt Larimore (optional)	

SESSION 7: PREPARING

REFLECT	Think through a live issue you are facing at work and come prepared to discuss it with the group.	20 mins
LISTEN	Bible through Workers' Eyes: 1 Peter	5 mins
READ	1 Peter 2:4-25, alert to how Peter's practical advice might play into a workplace environment.	30 mins
REFLECT	Where have you seen God at work?	

›SESSION 7‹

HOW CAN I TACKLE WORKPLACE ISSUES WITH BIBLICAL PRINCIPLES?

SESSION 7:
HOW CAN I TACKLE WORKPLACE ISSUES WITH BIBLICAL PRINCIPLES?

Over the past six sessions, we've looked at a range of ways in which we can bring biblical wisdom to bear on the opportunities and challenges we face at work. This session is an opportunity to try putting what we've learnt into practice by using some of those approaches – thinking relationally, influencing culture, reading the Bible with workers' eyes, using the 6M framework – to tackle first a case study and then some of our own live workplace situations.

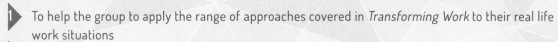

SESSION OBJECTIVES

1. To help the group to apply the range of approaches covered in *Transforming Work* to their real life work situations
2. To explore how to read New Testament letters with an alertness to the workplace context

SESSION MATERIALS

▶ *Transforming Work* DVD for Table Talk and Introduction to the Prayer of Examen videos

▶ Copies of Session 7 agenda

▶ Copies of 'Prayer of Examen' handout

▶ A box of Cadbury's Heroes (for example)

WELCOME & REVIEW   10 mins

Ask the group to share reflections since the last session:

▶ Where have you seen God at work?
▶ Has God been teaching you anything through your work since last time?

FEEDBACK – TAKING INTENTIONAL STEPS   20 mins

Discuss how people got on as they explored a new approach to workplace evangelism:

▶ Using the Pray4Life journey
▶ Implementing the 'Intentional Steps' discussed in the last session

CORE CONTENT: TACKLING WORKPLACE
ISSUES WITH BIBLICAL PRINCIPLES

50 mins

Take a few minutes to review with the group the approaches covered so far in the *Transforming Work* sessions: valuing good work; seeing what God is doing; working as God's children; discerning values and influencing culture; working relationally; and witnessing at work.

5 mins

Watch How Can I Tackle Workplace Issues with Biblical Principles? **(11 mins)**
You will need to pause the video twice to practise a case study.

20 mins

Tip: Take no more than five minutes for discussion at each pause point.

Ask group members to share their own 'live issues' in pairs, then work through them as real life case studies. This is an opportunity to revisit the 'One Big Question' that members shared in Session 2, or to identify a more recent issue, and explore creative solutions together. Allow pairs 10–15 minutes to discuss issues, then use the remaining time to feed back to the group.

25 mins

It will be helpful to keep the following questions in mind:
▶ Which of the 6Ms might be in play here?
▶ What do you think is the core issue underlying this problem?
▶ Is there a relational aspect to the issue?
▶ Can you discern the values underlying the issue?
▶ How might you pray in this circumstance?
▶ What biblical principles might be particularly relevant here?

BIBLE THROUGH WORKERS' EYES – 1 PETER

20 mins

This passage moves from the narrative style of the previous passages to one that contains specific encouragement and practical advice on Christian living. Peter refers to his audience as 'exiles', recognising that they were living out their Christian faith scattered geographically amongst towns and villages with a largely pagan culture.

In this session, we have been exploring how to use what we have learnt so far in *Transforming Work* to help the group to apply biblical principles to their working life. To see what principles this letter offers it's important first to be mindful of the situation for which it was initially written: what it might have meant to those early scattered Christians facing opposition. Then, in the light of this, think through how the group might respond as disciples when circumstances at work challenge their faith.

1 Peter 2:4-25

Use the following questions to aid the discussion of this passage as necessary:
▶ Verses 11-21 give practical advice on living as a Christian. What do the preceding verses say about the reason that we might want to do this?
▶ Looking at Peter's advice on living godly lives in a pagan society, what parallels can you see with your own context?
▶ What do you think of Peter's view of 'earthly authority' as it might apply to your workplace?
▶ How might the advice on enduring unjust punishment play into a modern workplace situation? Has that ever been your experience? How did you deal with it?

PRAYER

15 mins

The Prayer of Examen is a tool that can help you discern the voice and activity of God within your working day.

Watch Introduction to the Prayer of Examen (4 mins)

Invite the group to use the prayer to reflect on their working day: what's gone well or less well? Where have you engaged with God in your work and relationships? Where have you perhaps lost sight of God?

Tip: It may be helpful to put some quiet music on in the background during the time of reflection.

'The best decision anyone can ever make, at any point in life, in any circumstances, whoever they are, wherever they are, whatever they are, is to become a disciple of Jesus Christ. There is no better decision for a human being in this life, any human being.'
– Archbishop Justin Welby

JOURNEYING ON

5 mins

- ▶ Confirm the date for Session 8
- ▶ Remind people of the material to cover in between sessions
- ▶ Encourage the group to continue with personal journals and prayer between sessions
- ▶ Suggest people use the Prayer of Examen in their prayer partnerships/triplets

SESSION 7: GOING DEEPER

PRAY

READ/
LISTEN

Use the Prayer of Examen framework a few times each week	10 mins x3 per week
Ten at Work book or podcast by John Parmiter (optional)	

SESSION 8: PREPARING

REVIEW

LISTEN

READ

Consider your experience of *Transforming Work*. Summarise the main things God has been teaching you	1 hour
Bible through Workers' Eyes: Hebrews	5 mins
Hebrews 12:1-13, considering how you might remain fruitful for the long term	30 mins

·SESSION 8·

HOW CAN I REMAIN FRUITFUL OVER THE LONG-TERM?

SESSION 8:
▶ HOW CAN I REMAIN FRUITFUL ◀
OVER THE LONG-TERM?

Transforming Work aims to give people both a vision for how they can be fruitful at work as well as practical approaches to help them implement that vision. As the formal part of *Transforming Work* comes to a close, it's important to reflect on what they have learnt together and establish with the group how they might continue to grow in fruitfulness at work.

In this session there is much more time for Welcome and Review as this is the last time that the group will meet together. It is a chance for participants to reflect on what they have seen and how God has been working in their lives through the year. As the group hears from each other about the changes they have experienced, there's likely to be a growing sense of excitement. Acknowledge and celebrate these changes and take plenty of time. This will set things up well for the Table Talk discussion on how to be fruitful for the long-term.

SESSION OBJECTIVES

1. To celebrate what God has done in and through the group on the journey so far
2. To commit to pressing on, by establishing helpful habits that support long term fruitfulness
3. To practise reading New Testament letters through workers' eyes
4. To encourage others to lead a *Transforming Work* group

SESSION MATERIALS

▶ *Transforming Work* DVD for Table Talk and How Can I Pay it Forward? videos
▶ Copies of Session 8 agenda
▶ Box of Celebrations (or something else to celebrate with)

WELCOME & REVIEW   50 mins

Lead a discussion on the *Transforming Work* journey as a whole using the group's reflections.

▶ What are the main three things that you will take away with you at the end of this process?
▶ What has God been teaching you through your work over the whole year?
▶ Were there any significant moments when you saw God at work?

Tip: LICC would love to hear some of the stories coming out of your year of journeying together, to encourage others on the road and to make improvements based on your experience. Do get in touch with us via tw@licc.org.uk or via the app.

BIBLE THROUGH WORKERS' EYES - HEBREWS   20 mins

In our final session we are looking beyond *Transforming Work* towards following Jesus in the workplace over the long-term. We want to find ways that will help us to press on. The book of Hebrews does just that.

Hebrews was written to Jewish Christians who had successfully faced challenging opposition in the past, but whose confidence had then all but seeped away. They needed to be reminded of who it was they were following, and to recognise God's fatherly hand in the tough times they were experiencing. The previous chapter records a whole host of Old Testament 'faith heroes' who stood fast in the face of suffering even though they had yet to enjoy the fulfilled promise of Jesus.

Hebrews 12:1-13

What struck the group from their reading and reflection?

Discuss the passage, mindful of the call to be 'overcomers' as you seek to take forward what you've learnt together in *Transforming Work*.

Use these questions to aid discussion as needed:

▶ 'Since we are surrounded by such a great cloud of witnesses...' Do you have any modern day 'faith heroes'? Is there anybody who stands out to you in a workplace context as someone who is a true witness to Christ in what they say and do?

▶ Is there anything 'entangling' you as you seek to run the race? What would it mean to 'throw this off'?

▶ If you are facing hardships at work right now, can you see how they might produce a 'harvest of righteousness' in the long term? How do you need to respond for that to happen?

▶ How could we help each other in the race so that injuries we may pick up do not become disabilities (v13) but are healed?

CORE CONTENT:
REMAINING FRUITFUL OVER THE LONG-TERM   30 mins

Watch How Can I Remain Fruitful Over the Long-Term? **(11.5 mins)**

Recognising changes
In the video the team share some changes they have observed in their own work over the past year.
▶ In the light of what God has been teaching each person in the group, what has been changing in them over this year?

Committing to action
In the light of these changes, ask the group to write down their commitments, actions or goals for the coming year.

Tip: These can be recorded in 'Goals and Actions' in the *Transforming Work* app for future reference.

PRAYER & COMMISSIONING   15 mins

Many people have never been commissioned specifically for their everyday work. As the *Transforming Work* group comes to a formal close, this is a good opportunity to carry out a simple act of commissioning.

This can range from praying through the goals and actions that the group identified earlier, to something more symbolic like washing of hands to represent righteous working or anointing with oil to represent working in God's strength.

The words of Psalm 90:17 can be used as a group prayer:

**'May the favour of the Lord our God rest on us;
establish the work of our hands for us—
yes, establish the work of our hands.'**

Tip: You may like to hand out a symbol such as a small olive wooden cross as a reminder to the group of the journey they have been on and to encourage them in pressing forward.

JOURNEYING ON   5 mins

Watch How can I Pay it Forward? (2.5 mins)

▶ Suggest a date for a 6-month reunion as an opportunity to continue spurring one another on
▶ Encourage people to keep going with prayer partnerships and journalling to continue the process

SESSION 8: GOING DEEPER

READ   Practising the Presence of God at Work by Mark Greene   10 mins

WATCH   Victor's Story (2), noting his disciplines for fruitfulness   3 mins

► SECTION 2 ◄
SESSION MATERIALS

AGENDAS, HANDOUTS, AND EXERCISES

▶ WHY DOES WORK MATTER? ◀

GROUP INTRODUCTIONS

▶ Backgrounds, opportunities, and hopes

Notes:

HOW THE GROUP WILL OPERATE

▶ Core values
▶ *Transforming Work* as a journey
▶ What happens between sessions

Notes:

CORE CONTENT

▶ Work: The Bigger Picture
▶ Where have you seen God at work?

Notes:

PRAYER

▶ 6M Prayer Points

Notes:

BIBLE THROUGH WORKERS' EYES

▶ Introduction to Bible through Workers' Eyes

Notes:

JOURNEYING ON

SESSION 1 GOING DEEPER	PRAY		Pray using the 6Ms as a prompt	Ongoing
	WATCH	▶	Jay's Story, looking out for any of the 6Ms	5 mins
	READ	www	*Fruitfulness on the Frontline* by Mark Greene (optional)	
SESSION 2 PREPARING	EXERCISE		How Are You Doing at Work?	30 mins
	LISTEN	🔊	Bible through Workers' Eyes: Ruth & Boaz	5 mins
	READ		Ruth 2, noting any features that relate to a workplace situation	30 mins
	READ		Another Day, Another Dime by Mark Greene	20 mins
	REFLECT		Where have you seen God at work?	

THE 6MS
FRUITFULNESS AT WORK

The 6M framework, which you may already be familiar with from the *Fruitfulness on the Frontline* course, helps expand the vision of what it means to be a fruitful Christian in the workplace. It goes beyond simply being a nice person and having evangelistic conversations to help you see where God is already at work through you and to spot other opportunities in your everyday work. The Ms enhance one another and together increase fruitfulness.

When have you already...

M1   MODELLED GODLY CHARACTER?

This is the fruit of the Spirit in action – love, joy, peace, patience, kindness, goodness, faithfulness, gentleness, and self-control. When were these qualities particularly required? Or tested? Did you notice something different about your default response to situations?

M2   MADE GOOD WORK?

The work that you do matters in and of itself. Is your work on spec, on time, on budget? Giving your best is fundamental. But what does it mean to make good work with God? Are you conscious that you work for the Lord: in his image, in his strength, and to his glory?

M3   MINISTERED GRACE AND LOVE?

Here the attitudes of the heart and mind are brought to bear in specific situations and actions. How do you love someone who is feeling unwell or upset? How do you minister grace and love in more challenging situations? Or when a boss is unreasonable and fractious? In a redundancy situation when you have to 'pull the trigger'? Or when a colleague isn't pulling their weight?

M4   MOULDED CULTURE?

If culture is 'the way we do things around here', how do you influence the way that things are done in your workplace? How do the values behind the behaviours, attitudes, and norms of our workplaces measure up to Christian values? How might Christian values lead to different practices? Remember you can affect culture even if you are not in a position of power.

M5   BEEN A MOUTHPIECE FOR TRUTH AND JUSTICE?

There will be times when being a Christian at work means speaking up against things that are unfair, unhealthy, or untruthful, and speaking for things that are true, just, and good, whether it's about challenging major policy decisions or snuffing out gossip. This can be for your own benefit, or indeed on someone else's behalf (Philippians 2:3).

M6   BEEN A MESSENGER OF THE GOSPEL?

God loves your colleagues and wants them to know him better. As you pray for them and build relationships of trust, are you prepared to explain why you follow Jesus in a way they can appreciate? This may be through sharing a biblical perspective on a workplace issue, testifying to the way God has helped you in your work or, when the opportunity arises, engaging sensitively in a direct conversation about your beliefs.

HOW ARE YOU DOING AT WORK?

AN EXERCISE TO HELP YOU REFLECT ON YOUR WORK

During *Transforming Work*, we will look at a variety of aspects of your work and your workplace in some depth. This exercise will give you a snapshot of where you are at right now, helping identify your key issues, opportunities, and influences. It also provides a helpful benchmark that you can refer back to throughout your *Transforming Work* journey.

REFLECTIONS ON YOUR JOB

▶ Your job title/organisation:

▶ In a few words, can you summarise what your job involves?

▶ What are the key skills and character qualities required for the job?

▶ What are your major challenges right now?

▶ What are your hopes for the next year or so at work?

▶ How would you rate the quality of the products or services your organisation provides?

▶ How would you rate the quality of your own contribution?

▶ How would your bosses rate your performance?

▶ What aspects are you happy about?

▶ Where do you see opportunities for change in your performance?

REFLECTIONS ON YOUR INFLUENCES AND RESOURCES

▶ What resources have most influenced your attitude to work?

> ▶ Non-Christian influences e.g. your educational background, the media, workplace training programmes, government policy, etc.

> ▶ Overtly Christian influences e.g. a Christian book, a conference, a sermon series... or simply general input from your church

▶ Who do you consider to be your role models for working life?

▶ How would you describe your personal discipline of reading the Bible? To what extent do you feel that God's word helps to shape your working life?

▶ How would you describe your prayer life in relation to your work?

'By night I went out through the Valley Gate towards the Jackal Well and the Dung Gate, examining the walls of Jerusalem...'
- Nehemiah 2:13

MY OBSERVATIONS

Now look back over your answers.

▶ Does anything strike you? What is there to feel pleased about?

▶ Have any specific issues surfaced that you would particularly like to address?

▶ What do you think God may have been teaching you through your work in the last year or so? How has he been discipling you? Disciplining you?

What's the one big question that you would like the group to address this year?

Bring this question to your next group session.

▶ HOW CAN I DO GOOD WORK? ◀

WELCOME & REVIEW

▶ Where have you seen God at work?	Notes:

FEEDBACK

▶ 'How Are You Doing at Work?' reflections	Notes:

CORE CONTENT

Doing good work ▶ in God's ways ▶ in God's strength ▶ to God's glory	Notes:

BIBLE THROUGH WORKERS' EYES

▶ Ruth & Boaz	Notes:

PRAYER

▶ Big questions	Notes:

JOURNEYING ON

SESSION 2 GOING DEEPER	WATCH ▶	Sarah's Story, observing how she works in God's image	5 mins
	WATCH ▶	Sheona's Story, noting how God prepared her for good work	5 mins
	READ 📖	*Every Good Endeavour* by Tim Keller & Katherine Leary Alsdorf (optional)	
SESSION 3 PREPARING	EXERCISE ✏️	How Well are you Flourishing? Note that you will need to do part of this exercise alongside a close friend/spouse	20 mins
	WATCH ▶	Marion's Story, noting God's interest in her work	5 mins
	LISTEN 🔊	Bible through Workers' Eyes: Joseph	5 mins
	READ 📖	Genesis 39-45, with alertness to the workplace	40 mins
	REFLECT ✏️	Where have you seen God at work?	

HOW WELL ARE YOU FLOURISHING?

An exercise to help you think about whether you are thriving at the moment.

Complete page one by yourself and then give page two to a good friend or partner to complete, then compare the scores.

Score yourself against the following statements on a scale of 1 to 10.
10 is 'yes' and great, 1 is 'no' and awful.

1   I get about the right amount of sleep

2   I get about the right amount of time for family / key relationships

3   I work about the right amount of time

4   I have enough uninterrupted time on my own for reflection

5   I get to do the things that refresh me reasonably often

6   My lifestyle allows me to stay reasonably healthy

7   I feel my pace of life suits me – I don't need to escape

8   I feel at peace about the future

9   I have a good relationship with God

10   I am secure in who I am and am not driven by what other people think of me

11   I know the meaning and purpose of my life

12   There's another person who knows me well and to whom I can open up about my life

TOTAL
(out of 120)

Are there particular things that strike you?

HOW WELL ARE YOU FLOURISHING?
FRIEND'S VERSION

Score them as honestly as possible on a scale of 1 to 10.
10 is 'yes' and great, 1 is 'no' and awful.

1 X gets about the right amount of sleep

2 X gets about the right amount of time for family / key relationships

3 X works about the right amount of time

4 X has enough uninterrupted time by themselves for reflection

5 X gets to do the things that refresh them reasonably often

6 X's lifestyle allows them to stay reasonably healthy

7 X's pace of life suits them – they don't need to escape

8 X feels at peace about the future

9 X has a good relationship with God

10 X is secure in who they are and is not driven by what other people think of them

11 X knows the meaning and purpose of their life

12 There's another person who knows X well and to whom X can open up

TOTAL
(out of 120)

How do these scores compare to the scores you gave yourself?

▶ HOW CAN I FLOURISH AT WORK? ◀

WELCOME & REVIEW

| ▶ Where have you seen God at work? | Notes: |

FEEDBACK

| ▶ What did you learn from the 'How Well Are You Flourishing?' exercise? | Notes: |

CORE CONTENT

| ▶ Flourishing at work | Notes: |

BIBLE THROUGH WORKERS' EYES

| ▶ Genesis 39-45 | Notes: |

PRAYER

| ▶ Pressure points and kingdom purpose | Notes: |

JOURNEYING ON

SESSION 3 GOING DEEPER	WATCH ▶	Living an Integrated Life interview with Paul Valler	5 mins
	READ 🌐	*Get a Life* by Paul Valler (optional)	
SESSION 4 PREPARING	LISTEN 🔊	Bible through Workers' Eyes: Jehoshaphat	5 mins
	READ 📖	2 Chronicles 17-20 thinking about how Jehoshaphat went about influencing the culture in Judah through his role as ruler	40 mins
	WATCH ▶	Anita's Story, looking out for her influence on workplace culture	5 mins
	REFLECT ✏	Where have you seen God at work?	

▶ HOW CAN I INFLUENCE THE CULTURE ◀
OF MY WORKPLACE?

WELCOME & REVIEW

▶ Where have you seen God at work?

Notes:

FEEDBACK

▶ 'Living an Integrated Life' challenges and encouragements

Notes:

BIBLE THROUGH WORKERS' EYES

▶ 2 Chronicles 17-20

Notes:

CORE CONTENT

▶ Influencing the culture of my workplace

Notes:

PRAYER

▶ Making one-degree shifts in culture

Notes:

JOURNEYING ON

SESSION 4 GOING DEEPER	DO	One-degree shifts in your workplace	Ongoing
	WATCH	Counter-Cultural Working interview with Jago Wynne	5 mins
	READ	William's Story by Mark Greene	20 mins
	READ	*Culture Making* by Andy Crouch (optional)	
SESSION 5 PREPARING	LISTEN	Bible through Workers' Eyes: Over to You	5 mins
	READ	Your regular Bible passages, but with a specific alertness to your work context	Daily
	REFLECT	Where have you seen God at work?	

WHAT'S THE CULTURE OF MY WORKPLACE?

An exercise to help you discern what shapes your workplace culture and start to influence it

1   If my workplace was a _____ what would it be and why?

▶ Picture your organisation as an animal or a car. What sort of animal/car would it be?

▶ Work in pairs to discuss why you pictured it like that and be ready to share with the group.

2   Thinking about your workplace...

▶ What about your workplace brings you joy or helps you to flourish?

▶ What about your workplace frustrates you or makes you angry?

3   Reflect

▶ Spend a few minutes thinking about your answers to questions 1 and 2. What do they tell you about the values in your workplace?

WATCH 'HOW CAN I INFLUENCE THE CULTURE OF MY WORKPLACE?'

4   What in your workplace resonates with biblical values and what doesn't?

▶ Which of the features of your workplace identified in questions 1 and 2 align with biblical values and which cut across them?

Some examples of biblical values: serving others, valuing people, truth telling, showing love, working with righteousness, demonstrating justice, giving and receiving joy, or making peace.

ALIGNS WITH
BIBLICAL VALUES

CUTS ACROSS
BIBLICAL VALUES

5   Which one-degree shifts (small practical steps) could you make with God's help to reinforce good values and improve poor ones?

REINFORCING
GOOD VALUES

IMPROVING
POOR VALUES

▶ HOW CAN I IMPROVE RELATIONSHIPS ◀ AT WORK?

WELCOME & REVIEW

▶ Where have you seen God at work?

Notes:

FEEDBACK

▶ Making one-degree shifts

Notes:

BIBLE THROUGH WORKERS' EYES

▶ Reflections on personal Bible reading

Notes:

CORE CONTENT

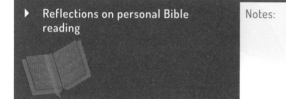

▶ Improving workplace relationships

Notes:

PRAYER

▶ Workplace relationships

Notes:

JOURNEYING ON

SESSION 5 GOING DEEPER	DO	Take some intentional steps towards improving your workplace relationships	Daily
	WATCH	Mel's Story, looking out for what she brings to workplace relationships	5 mins
	WATCH	John's Story (1)	5 mins
	READ	Life Through the Relational Lens by Mark Greene	20 mins
	READ	*The Relational Manager* by Michael Schluter and David John Lee (optional)	
SESSION 6 PREPARING	LISTEN	Bible through Workers' Eyes: Jesus & His Disciples	5 mins
	READ	John 1:29-51, with alertness to introducing others to Jesus	30 mins
	WATCH	Neil's Stories	10 mins
	WATCH	Victor's Story (1)	5 mins
	REFLECT	Where have you seen God at work?	

HOW ARE MY WORKPLACE RELATIONSHIPS?

An exercise to help you look at the health of your workplace relationships

1 A QUICK THREE-STEP HEALTH CHECK

A **WHO do you relate to at work?**

Write down your most significant workplace relationships.

MY MOST SIGNIFICANT WORKPLACE RELATIONSHIPS

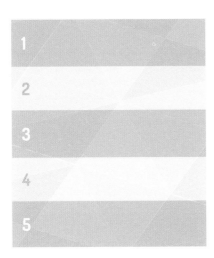

B **HOW healthy are those relationships?**

Rate the quality of your workplace relationships (above) on the table below. You might want to think about some of the following characteristics of a healthy relationship to help you position them:

- ▶ Transparency — you both share all information that's relevant (personal if appropriate)
- ▶ Time — you give each other enough time
- ▶ Trust — there is good will and support on both sides

IN GOOD SHAPE   **OK**   **NOT GOOD**

C WHY do you think they are like that?

Discuss in pairs what makes the good relationships work well, and what causes the other relationships to be poor. Write down those that stand out to you as particularly important.

RELATIONSHIP
ENHANCERS

RELATIONSHIP
HARMERS

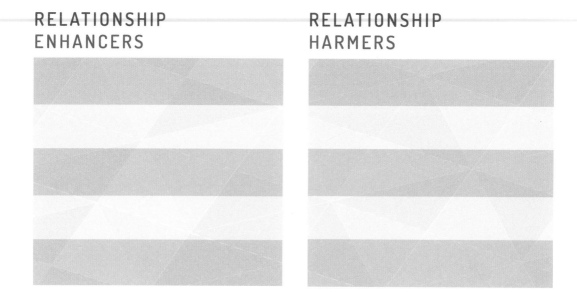

WATCH 'HOW CAN I IMPROVE RELATIONSHIPS AT WORK?'

2 HOW COULD YOU IMPROVE YOUR WORKPLACE RELATIONSHIPS?

Looking at your answers above, did the video give you any further ideas for improving a poor relationship at work?

Write down some specific actions you could take to make a real difference.

▶ HOW CAN I SHARE MY FAITH AT WORK? ◀

WELCOME & REVIEW

▶ Where have you seen God at work?	Notes:

FEEDBACK

▶ Stories of relational change	Notes:

CORE CONTENT

▶ Sharing faith at work	Notes:

PRAYER & INTENTIONAL STEPS

▶ Praying for colleagues	Notes:

BIBLE THROUGH WORKERS' EYES

▶ John 1:29-51	Notes:

JOURNEYING ON

SESSION 6 GOING DEEPER	PRAY		Sign-up in-app to the Pray4Life prayer journey. You'll receive an email of just 140 characters for 40 days to help you pray for three people	Daily
	DO		Review your possible next steps identified in the exercise and start to put some of them into practice	
	WATCH		Jeremy's Story and Wayne's Story, noting pathways forward	10 mins
	WATCH		John's Story (2)	5 mins
	READ		*Workplace Grace* by Bill Peel and Walt Larimore (optional)	
SESSION 7 PREPARING	REFLECT		Think through a live issue you are facing at work and come prepared to discuss it with the group	20 mins
	LISTEN		Bible through Workers' Eyes: 1 Peter	5 mins
	READ		1 Peter 2:4-25, alert to how Peter's practical advice might play into a workplace environment	30 mins
	REFLECT		Where have you seen God at work?	

INTENTIONAL STEPS: SHARING FAITH

Pick one workplace contact that you feel God is laying on your heart at this time. With this person in mind, complete the first four questions before watching the video with your group.

THE CURRENT STATE OF PLAY

▶ How would you describe this person generally?

▶ What can you see is important to this person?

▶ What do you think they believe about God?

▶ What is your relationship with them like?

POSSIBLE NEXT STEPS

▶ Any specific insights from your prayer time:

▶ How could you get to know this person better?

▶ Who might commit to praying for them with you?

▶ What could you do to bless this person practically?

▶ What would help you to be prepared for opportunities?

▶ One thing I will commit to doing next:

▶ HOW CAN I TACKLE WORKPLACE ISSUES ◀
WITH BIBLICAL PRINCIPLES?

WELCOME & REVIEW

▶ Where have you seen God at work?	Notes:

FEEDBACK

▶ Taking intentional steps	Notes:

CORE CONTENT

▶ Tackling workplace issues with biblical principles	Notes:

BIBLE THROUGH WORKERS' EYES

▶ 1 Peter 2:4-25	Notes:

PRAYER

▶ Growing in godly character: The Prayer of Examen	Notes:

JOURNEYING ON

SESSION 7 GOING DEEPER	PRAY		Use the Prayer of Examen framework a few times each week	10 mins x3 per week
	READ/ LISTEN		*Ten at Work* book or podcast by John Parmiter (optional)	
SESSION 8 PREPARING	REVIEW		Consider your experience of *Transforming Work*. Summarise the main things God has been teaching you	1 hour
	LISTEN		Bible through Workers' Eyes: Hebrews	5 mins
	READ		Hebrews 12:1-13, considering how you might remain fruitful for the long term.	30 mins

THE PRAYER OF EXAMEN
FOR WORKERS

DISCERNING THE VOICE AND ACTIVITY OF GOD WITHIN THE FLOW OF THE DAY

'And this is my prayer; that your love may abound more and more in knowledge and depth of insight, so that you may be able to discern what is best and may be pure and blameless until the day of Christ, filled with the fruit of righteousness that comes through Jesus Christ – to the glory and praise of God.'
Philippians 1:9-11

Examen is a daily exercise initiated by Ignatius some 500 years ago to help people to serve God better through reflection. It has five simple steps and takes about 10 minutes to complete.

1. STILLNESS

Relax. Allow the tensions of the day to dissipate, and recognise that you are in God's presence.

2. THANKFULNESS

Look at your day with gratitude for the gifts God has given you: a task completed, a relationship deepened, progress made on a project, customers served well.

3. INSPIRATION

Ask the Holy Spirit to give you some insight into the events and emotions of the day.

4. REVIEW AND REFLECTION

Reflect peacefully on what has been happening to you, in you, and through you today. Having asked God for the help of his Holy Spirit, trust that he will show you whatever he wants you to see. You may find a few of the following questions useful in prompting your reflection.

▶ Have you learned anything today about God and his ways, in the everyday events of living and working?

▶ Where did you meet him in the ups and downs: fears, joys, misunderstandings, weariness, exhilaration?

▶ Where did you feel the absence of God in any part of your day? If so, why do you think that was?

▶ Where did you feel God prompting you, nudging you in any particular way? How did you respond?

▶ How were your moods today? e.g. What made you feel peaceful? When did you experience unease or turmoil? Reflect on what it was that seemed to make you react in these ways, and open up your feelings to God for affirmation or healing.

▶ Notice your habits and patterns in the day. Which positive ones would you seek to reinforce? Which negative ones could you lay down with God's help?

▶ Where did you get the opportunity to live out one or more of the 6Ms today? How did you respond? Would you do anything differently tomorrow?

5. RECONCILIATION AND RESOLVE

In your reflection you may have noticed both moments to celebrate and other moments that caused you sorrow.

▶ Thank God for those things that went well, and ask him to show more of his love to others through you.

▶ Where it seems your response to God or others was lacking, ask for (and be confident in) forgiveness, and rejoice at God's deep desire to help you love him and others well.

▶ Finally, look forward to tomorrow. Ask for sensitivity to recognise God's promptings in the day and courage and wisdom to act upon them. Pray for an open heart in a busy and pressured working environment, and open hands to minister to those around you as opportunities arise. If you already know that you will be facing challenging situations, ask for wisdom and a right heart attitude. Invite God to be with you in each situation.

▶ HOW CAN I REMAIN FRUITFUL OVER THE ◀ LONG-TERM?

WELCOME & REVIEW

▶ What has God been teaching you in and through your work over the course of *Transforming Work*?

Notes:

BIBLE THROUGH WORKERS' EYES

▶ Hebrews 12:1-13

Notes:

CORE CONTENT

▶ Remaining fruitful over the long-term
▶ Recognising changes
▶ Committing to action

Notes:

PRAYER

▶ Commissioning

Notes:

JOURNEYING ON

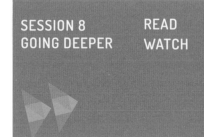

SESSION 8 GOING DEEPER	READ WATCH		Practising the Presence of God at Work by Mark Greene	10 mins
			Victor's Story (2), noting his disciplines for fruitfulness	5 mins

If you would like to share something – a story, an idea, a discovery – about faith at work, please email us at tw@licc.org.uk. We promise to treasure your story and make contact.

TRANSFORMING
WORK

▶ SECTION 3 ◀

GETTING GOING

GETTING GOING

We're so excited that you're planning to run a *Transforming Work* group. We trust that it will be a hugely rewarding experience for you as you see people recognising, perhaps for the first time, the significance of their own work to God, growing in fruitfulness, and seeing change in their workplaces.

We have prepared six short introductory videos which are in the 'Extras' section of the DVD. These are optional but are designed to help you get to grips with *Transforming Work* and make the most of your experience leading a group. You might find it best to run through the videos with your co-leader and/or other leaders if multiple groups are beginning simultaneously in your church or organisation. Some of the videos also come with helpful exercises. Even if you do them all at once, it should take no more than two hours to work though the videos and exercises and discuss the points raised.

1 WORK: THE BIGGER PICTURE - MARK GREENE

This looks at why the workplace matters to God and casts the vision for *Transforming Work*. It forms part of Session 1 and so will eventually be watched by your group, but it provides a helpful foundation for this introductory material.

▶ Session Video:
10 minutes

2 HOW TO ACCOMPANY A GROUP - RUTH WALKER

An introduction to the *Transforming Work* course and your role as a group leader. After watching this video, use the reflection exercise What Kind of Leader are You? on page 67.

▶ Training Video:
5 minutes
▶ Exercise:
15 minutes

3 GETTING THE MOST FROM PEOPLE'S STORIES - RUTH WALKER

A practical exercise to help you guide the group in seeing where God is at work, as they share opportunities and challenges. The case study exercise is on page 70 for reference.

▶ Training Video:
5+5 minutes
▶ Exercise:
20 minutes

4 BIBLE THROUGH WORKERS' EYES - MARK GREENE

This core video offers a compelling overview of how so much of the Bible addresses work issues directly and indirectly. Reading the Bible through Workers' Eyes is a key part of each *Transforming Work* session. The video also forms part of Session 1.

▶ Session Video:
5 minutes

5 INTRODUCING RUTH 2 THROUGH WORKERS' EYES - RUTH WALKER

This video takes you through a worked example of reading the Bible through Workers' Eyes using Ruth Chapter 2. This is the first passage that your group will study in preparation for Session 2.

▶ Training Video:
5+5 minutes
▶ Exercise:
10 minutes

6 Q&A FOR LEADING A TRANSFORMING WORK GROUP - RUTH WALKER

Ruth Walker answers some common questions from people who have led a *Transforming Work* group.

▶ Training Video:
5 minutes

REFLECTION EXERCISE:
WHAT KIND OF LEADER ARE YOU?

If you've led a discussion or Bible study group before, you will probably have all the skills you need. A distinctive feature of *Transforming Work* is that the leader does not act as the expert. Rather, they learn along with the group while encouraging everyone to participate by gently guiding discussion and asking open questions. As with any group the leader sets the pace for learning, responding to what is said in the group discussion and encouraging the group to push on further.

The following questions are designed to help you reflect on your style of leading, and will help you consider how you are able to apply and adapt the skills you already have to the particular challenges of a *Transforming Work* group.

COVERING THE MATERIAL

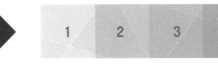

I anticipate the questions and issues that might arise so that I am able to keep the session on track

| 1 | 2 | 3 | 4 | 5 |

I am good at discerning whether an unexpected question is fruitful for the group to pursue

| 1 | 2 | 3 | 4 | 5 |

▶ **Reflect:** How do you react when individuals want to move off the main topic?

If someone raises an issue, you need to discern if this is something that the whole group wants to discuss. It can be helpful to say to the group: 'If we carry on this conversation it may mean we have to leave one of the other agenda items'. Then ask the group if they want to continue with this discussion, or suggest how long you will give this conversation. It may mean you have to find another way to pick up those topics you have had to leave to one side.

It is important that you are willing to adapt and be responsive to the needs of participants, while ensuring that important material is covered at some stage.

RESPONDING TO ISSUES

I like to be realistic with people, helping them to confront any issues they are facing

| 1 | 2 | 3 | 4 | 5 |

When people are facing issues, I like to help them look at possibilities not problems

| 1 | 2 | 3 | 4 | 5 |

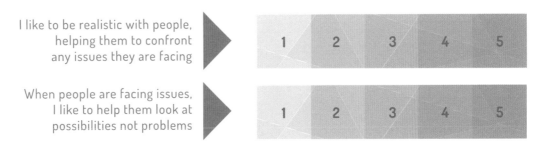

▶ **Reflect:** How do you help people when they raise issues or problems?

In *Transforming Work* we are helping people to see how God is at work in their lives. It can be helpful to encourage people to look at possibilities rather than problems. Stories from the Bible and stories of Christians in different situations can contribute to the conversation. These examples will help group members to see their own stories in fresh ways, to dig deeper into their faith at work, and to learn to articulate their own faith stories.

HEARING ONE ANOTHER

I listen to people, using questions to make sure they've fully communicated their thoughts to the group

| 1 | 2 | 3 | 4 | 5 |

I listen, checking for my understanding, but let the group do most of the talking

| 1 | 2 | 3 | 4 | 5 |

▶ Reflect: How are your listening skills?

Open ended questions tend to encourage people to talk about whatever is important to them – the Who, What, Why, Where, When, and How? questions. You could also try framing your questions with phrases like 'Would you tell me more about...?' or 'Could you help me understand...?' Remember to maintain eye contact, nodding and avoiding interrupting. Show that you have heard by acknowledging, summarising, or rephrasing what group members are saying. If you model these behaviours as a leader, it will help you to manage group participation better – especially for those who don't listen but rather tend to dominate.

KEEPING CONFIDENCES

I keep stories to myself, however encouraging they might be to others

| 1 | 2 | 3 | 4 | 5 |

I like to share stories I have heard, using names to make them credible

| 1 | 2 | 3 | 4 | 5 |

▶ Reflect: Do you easily keep confidences?

There can be a fine line between sharing helpful stories and breaking a confidence. If you think a story would be helpful to share, make sure you have permission first. As a group you will set guidelines for confidentiality, and as a leader you need to model that. A group is damaged if they feel that their private stories will be told in public places.

OPENING UP

I prefer to keep my challenges to myself, so that I don't appear to dominate

| 1 | 2 | 3 | 4 | 5 |

I'm willing to share my story as it helps others to open up

| 1 | 2 | 3 | 4 | 5 |

▶ Reflect: How do you demonstrate that you're also learning to apply the principles in the course to your own working life?

Being authentic about your walk with God at work will help others see that you are continuing to work out your faith rather than having all the answers. It is helpful to admit when you have struggled as well as when you have rejoiced or been surprised. Your stories should not dominate the group but they can really help to build trust and honesty within the group.

USING THE BIBLE

I tend to look to good common-sense workplace practice to deal with situations

| 1 | 2 | 3 | 4 | 5 |

I tend to look to the Bible to illuminate situations and workplace issues

| 1 | 2 | 3 | 4 | 5 |

▶ **Reflect**: How do you use the Bible as a source of wisdom and insight?

While 'common sense' is important, the Bible can illuminate work situations and give us everyday examples to follow. 'Introducing Ruth 2 through Workers' Eyes' gives an example of how to do this. As you practise reading the Bible through workers' eyes you will grow in biblical wisdom yourself and be able to help others to do this as well.

PRAYING FOR THE GROUP

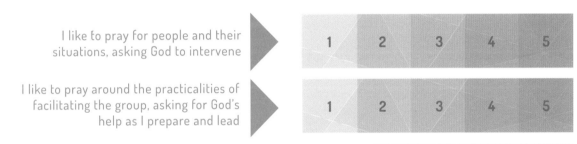

I like to pray for people and their situations, asking God to intervene

| 1 | 2 | 3 | 4 | 5 |

I like to pray around the practicalities of facilitating the group, asking for God's help as I prepare and lead

| 1 | 2 | 3 | 4 | 5 |

▶ Reflect: How will you keep the participants as well as your preparation in your prayers?

There is no right or wrong way to pray. We do encourage group leaders to pray very specifically for those in their group and their workplaces, as well as for the running of the group. It helps you remember their issues and it upholds the individuals as they live out their faith. As you see God answer prayer, you will be encouraged as you accompany the group.

EXERCISE:

GETTING THE MOST FROM PEOPLE'S STORIES – A CASE STUDY

This forms part of the 'Getting Going' video 3. Read through the 'Craig' case study. Think about how you might handle the conversation, and what you would say to Craig yourself, and write it down.

> Craig is a member of your group. He tends to be quiet and thoughtful. He is well liked by other members of the group. He volunteers this story when the group shares where they have seen God at work. He isn't sure that he has seen God but he is asking you to help make sense of what is going on in his workplace.
>
> 'I've started a new job in a shop but because I was bullied badly in my last job for being a Christian, I've decided I won't say anything about my faith in Jesus. I'm in sales and the targets are everything, so I'm trying to be reasonable and not too pushy with clients. I'm keen to achieve and I am managing to hit my targets, but I feel under pressure to do better, especially with the other men in the sales team. There is a lot of sexual innuendo in the conversation that I am uncomfortable about. There are several youngish girls who I work alongside so I'm careful not to join in the sexually explicit chat. I think that is a bad way to speak of them. I'm worried about going on the work's night out which will inevitably be wild. I feel like a total failure and that I'm not being a good witness at all.'

▶ How would you encourage Craig to have eyes to see where God is already using him and where he is already being fruitful?

NOTES:

JOURNEYING ON

Fruitfulness on the Frontline – Eight-session group **DVD**. In this liberating resource, Mark Greene offers a fresh, simple framework for discovering a rich variety of ways in which God might work in and through us right where we are. Biblical teaching, real-life stories, a downloadable discussion guide, and bags of free support material are included.

Fruitfulness on the Frontline – A **book** complementing the frontline DVD courses which explores the 6M framework in greater depth: modelling godly character; making good work; ministering grace and love; moulding culture; being a mouthpiece for truth and justice; being a messenger of the gospel. Combining biblical reflection and a rich range of contemporary examples, you'll not only have a sense of how God might work in you right where you are but a greater awareness of how he already has.

Thank God it's Monday – Fun, fast, and full of stories, the **fourth** edition of this contemporary classic offers a compelling vision for work, providing biblical perspectives and examples on a range of key topics – the value of work, ministry and witness at work, ethics, authority, ambition, and work-home integration.

Executive Toolbox – A course for those with mid- to senior-level executive responsibilities. Three 24-hour workshops on leading workplace culture change, building strong relationships, and using power and authority well.

Prayer Journeys – Our 40-day prayer journeys give you quick, easy, and fresh ways to pray in and for your everyday situations. We'll send you daily prompts to spark your imagination, encouraging you to pray – however briefly – with renewed energy, creativity, and faith that God's purposes will be worked out in your life.

Find out more at licc.org.uk

ABOUT LICC

Our focus at LICC is on empowering Christians to make a difference in God's world, and envisioning and equipping church leaders to help them do it.

Founded by John Stott in 1982, and now led by Mark Greene, LICC's growing team seeks to combine biblical wisdom, cultural insight, and practical ideas to offer individuals and ministers a wide range of resources. We speak, run courses and workshops, and offer consultancy to churches. And if you click on our website you'll find a trove of free material – clips, articles, downloads – as well as simple sign-ups for our themed prayer journeys and our punchy weekly emails – Word for the Week and Connecting with Culture.

Explore more at licc.org.uk.

DVD CONTENTS

SESSION 1

WHY DOES WORK MATTER?
- ▶ Work: The Bigger Picture
- ▶ Where Have you Seen God at Work?
- ▶ Bible through Workers' Eyes

SESSION 2

HOW CAN I DO GOOD WORK?
- ▶ How Can I Do Good Work?

SESSION 3

HOW CAN I FLOURISH AT WORK?
- ▶ How Can I Flourish at Work?

SESSION 4

HOW CAN I INFLUENCE THE CULTURE OF MY WORKPLACE?
- ▶ How Can I Influence the Culture of my Workplace?
- ▶ Chris' Story

SESSION 5

HOW CAN I IMPROVE RELATIONSHIPS AT WORK?
- ▶ How Can I Improve Relationships at Work?
- ▶ Laura's Story

SESSION 6

HOW CAN I SHARE MY FAITH AT WORK?
- ▶ How Can I Share my Faith at Work?

SESSION 7

HOW CAN I TACKLE WORKPLACE ISSUES WITH BIBLICAL PRINCIPLES?
- ▶ How Can I Tackle Workplace Issues with Biblical Principles?
- ▶ Introduction to the Prayer of Examen

SESSION 8

HOW CAN I REMAIN FRUITFUL OVER THE LONG-TERM?
- ▶ How Can I Remain Fruitful Over the Long-Term?
- ▶ How Can I Pay it Forward?

EXTRAS

PROMOS
- ▶ *Transforming Work* Promo

GETTING GOING
- ▶ 1) Work: The Bigger Picture
- ▶ 2) How to Accompany a Group
- ▶ 3) Getting the Most from People's Stories
- ▶ 4) Bible through Workers' Eyes
- ▶ 5) Introducing Ruth 2 through Workers' Eyes
- ▶ 6) Q&A for Leading a *Transforming Work* Group

STORIES & INTERVIEWS
- ▶ Anita's Story
- ▶ Jay's Story
- ▶ Jeremy's Story
- ▶ Marion's Story
- ▶ Mel's Story
- ▶ Neil's Stories
- ▶ Sarah's Story
- ▶ Sheona's Story
- ▶ John's Story (1)
- ▶ John's Story (2)
- ▶ Victor's Story (1)
- ▶ Victor's Story (2)
- ▶ Wayne's Story
- ▶ Interview: Counter-Cultural Working
- ▶ Interview: Living an Integrated Life